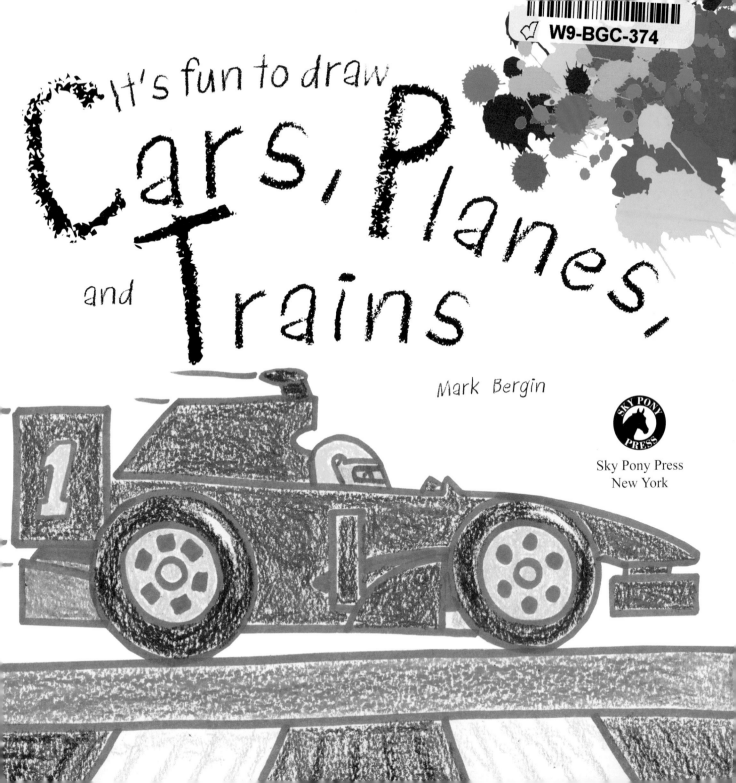

It's fun to draw

Cars, Planes, and Trains

Mark Bergin

Sky Pony Press
New York

Mark Bergin was born in Hastings, England. He has illustrated an award-winning series and written over twenty books. He has done many book designs, layouts, and storyboards in many styles including cartoon for numerous books, posters, and advertisements. He lives in Bexhill-on-Sea with his wife and three children.

HOW TO USE THIS BOOK:

Start by following the numbered splats on the left-hand page. These steps will ask you to add some lines to your drawing. The new lines are always drawn in red so you can see how the drawing builds from step to step. Read the "You can do it!" splats to learn about drawing and shading techniques you can use.

Sky Pony Press books may be purchased in bulk at special discounts for sales promotion, corporate gifts, fund-raising, or educational purposes. Special editions can also be created to specifications. For details, contact the Special Sales Department, Sky Pony Press, 307 West 36th Street, 11th Floor, New York, NY 10018 or info@skyhorsepublishing.com.

Sky Pony® is a registered trademark of Skyhorse Publishing, Inc.®, a Delaware corporation.

Visit our website at www.skyponypress.com.

10 9 8 7 6 5 4 3 2

Manufactured in China, September 2020
This product conforms to CPSIA 2008

Library of Congress Cataloging-in-Publication Data

Bergin, Mark, 1961-
It's fun to draw cars, planes, and trains / Mark Bergin.
pages cm
Summary: "This book is filled with fun and creative technique suggestions, using basic materials like markers, crayons, oil pastels, colored pencils, watercolor paint, and more to create vibrant machines of all kinds"-- Provided by publisher.
ISBN 978-1-63220-410-3 (paperback)
1. Vehicles in art--Juvenile literature. 2. Transportation in art--Juvenile literature. 3. Drawing--Technique--Juvenile literature. I. Title.
NC825.V45B47 2015
743'.8962904--dc23
2015007043

Cover illustration credit Mark Bergin

Contents

Sports car

 **1** Start with the main body of the car.

2 Add the wheels and a line for the ground.

Splat-a-fact
Sports cars have very fast acceleration.

You can do it!
Use a felt-tip marker for the lines. Add highlights with crayon, then brush colored ink over it.

3 Draw in the roof and the windows.

4 Add the driver and a spoiler at the back of the car.

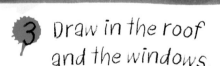

5 Add finishing details.

Aerobatic plane

1 Start by drawing the plane's fuselage (body).

2 Draw in the canopy and tail fin.

you can do it!
Use a felt-tip marker for the lines and add color using colored pencils.

splat-a-fact
Aerobatic planes perform acrobatic maneuvers in formation.

3 Draw in the wings.

4 Add the pilot and tail fin number.

5 Add finishing details and motion lines.

Steam locomotive

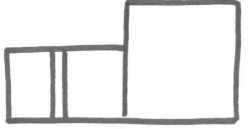

1 Start by drawing the main body of the locomotive.

you can do it!
Use a felt-tip marker for the lines. Use colored oil pastels to add color.

2 Add the chimney, dome, and roof.

3 Draw in the wheels. Add lines for the railway track.

splat-a-fact
Steam power drives the locomotive's wheels.

4 Add the driver and the finishing details.

8

9

Learjet

1 Draw the jet's fuselage with a big black dot for the nose.

2 Draw in the windshield.

you can do it!

Use a felt-tip marker for the lines. Use crayons for detail, then paint on top—the wax will act as a resistant.

3 Draw in the twin jet engines.

splat-a-fact
Learjets are small passenger planes.

4 Draw in the wings.

5 Draw in the pilots and the tail.

NASCAR

1 Start with the body of the car.

2 Add the roof and wheels.

3 Add the spoiler, lights, bumpers, and hubcaps.

Splat-a-fact
NASCAR stands for National Association for Stock Car Auto Racing.

4 Add the driver and all finishing details.

Electric train

MAKE SURE AN ADULT HELPS YOU WHEN USING SCISSORS!

1 Start by cutting out the main body of the train.

splat-a-fact

The fastest trains are powered by electricity.

2 Cut out four wheels, the rail track, and the nose part. Glue down.

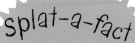

3 Cut out the windshield, side panel, and red stripe. Glue down.

you can do it!

Cut out the shapes from colored paper and glue in place. Use a felt-tip marker for details.

4 Cut out a light and windows, then glue down. Draw in the driver and any other remaining details.

Spitfire

1 Start with an oval for the Spitfire's fuselage and a circle for the propeller cap.

2 Draw in the cockpit and the pilot.

splat-a-fact

The Spitfire was a British fighter aircraft from World War II.

3 Draw in the engine parts.

4 Draw in the wings.

5 Draw in the horizontal and vertical stabilizers.

Beetle

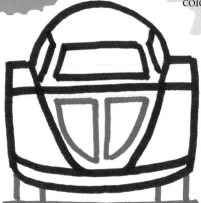

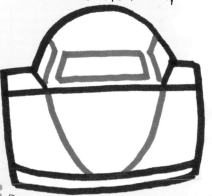

1 Start by drawing the car's body and roof.

2 Draw in the rear wheel arches and the bumper.

3 Draw in the windows and the hood.

4 Add detail to the hood and draw in the wheels.

5 Add the headlights, side mirrors, and windshield reflection.

splat-a-fact
The beetle was one of the first rear-engined cars.

You can do it!
Draw the lines with a felt-tip marker and glue down torn tissue paper for color.

Freight train

1 Start by drawing the main body of the train.

2 Draw in the undercarriage.

3 Add the windows and side panels.

4 Draw in the headlight, horn, and front grill. Add the driver.

Pitts Special

1 Start by drawing the main shape of the plane.

Splat-a-fact
The Pitts Special is an aerobatic biplane used for high speed stunts and racing.

2 Draw in the pilot, the horizontal stabilizer, and a lightning flash.

3 Draw in the wings and add a propeller.

you can do it!
Use a felt-tip marker for the lines. Add color with crayons, using different kinds of scribbly marks to add variety. Paint over with a watercolor wash.

4 Draw in the undercarriage.

F1 car

1 Start by drawing the body and rear wing of the car.

2 Draw in the wheels, rear section, and a line for the ground.

you can do it!
Use a felt-tip marker for the lines and add color using colored pencils.

3 Draw in the front wing and the side and top engine air intakes.

Splat-a-fact
The first ever Formula One race was held in 1950.

4 Draw in wheel nuts and camera mount. Add the driver.

Tank engine

1 Start with the main body of the tank engine.

2 Draw in the roof, sides, and undercarriage.

3 Draw in a chimney, boiler, and windows.

splat-a-fact
Tank engines are compact versions of steam locomotives.

4 Add the wheels, boiler, bumper, and coupling details.

you can do it!
Use a felt-tip marker for the lines and add color with watercolor paints. Use a sponge to dab on some color for added texture.

5 Draw in the tunnel, driver, and rails. Add a puff of smoke from the chimney.

26

Glider

1 Start with the glider's curved fuselage.

2 Draw in the cockpit and the pilot.

3 Draw in the vertical stabilizer and the undercarriage hatch.

You can do it!

Use a felt-tip marker for the lines and color in with colored pencils. Blend the pencils with your fingers.

Splat-a-fact

Gliders have no engine. Thermals (hot air rising from the ground) carry gliders up through the air.

4 Add the wing, tail stripe, back light, and top section of the vertical stabilizer.

Hot rod

1 Start by drawing the car body.

You can do it!
Use a felt-tip marker for the lines and add color using colored ink washes.

2 Draw in the wheels, wheel arches, and the ground.

3 Draw in the windows and the bumpers. Add the driver.

4 Add the headlights, big engine, and flame decoration.

Index